Weather

Catriona Clarke
Designed by Andrea Slane
Illustrated by Kuo Kang Chen

Additional illustrations by Tim Haggerty
Weather consultant: Dr. Roger Trend, University of Exeter
Reading consultant: Alison Kelly, Roehampton University

Contents

3   Rain or shine

4   What is weather?

6   Water on the move

8   Clouding over

10   Icy crystals

12   Electric skies

14   Great balls of ice

16   Wild wind

18   Terrible twisters

20   Weather scientists

22   Animal magic

24   Hot and cold

26   Weird weather

28   Heating up?

30   Glossary of weather words

31   Websites to visit

32   Index

Rain or shine

The weather can be sunny, rainy, windy or snowy. Every kind of weather is happening somewhere in the world right now.

This is a snowstorm in New York, USA.

What is weather?

The weather is caused by three main things: heat, water and air.

The Sun gives out heat which warms the Earth.

Water makes clouds and rain. It also makes fog, hail and snow.

Air is always moving around. This is what makes the wind blow.

The Earth is wrapped in a thick blanket of air called the atmosphere. This is where weather happens.

From space, the atmosphere looks like a hazy blue ring around the Earth. The white swirls are clouds.

Water on the move

Water is always moving between the sea, the air and the land. This is called the water cycle.

1. The Sun warms the water in the sea and turns it into an invisible gas.

2. The gas rises and turns into tiny droplets of water, making clouds.

The rain that falls on you may have
fallen on a dinosaur millions of years ago.

3. The tiny droplets
bump into each other
and join together to
make bigger drops.

4. When the drops
of water become
heavy enough they
fall as rain.

5. Rivers carry
the rainwater back
to the sea. The water
cycle begins again.

Clouding over

Different types of clouds mean there will be different kinds of weather.

Puffy white cumulus clouds usually mean that good weather is coming.

Stratus clouds cover the sky. This means that there might be fog or drizzle.

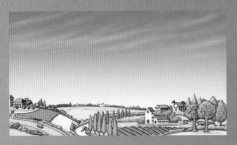

Wispy cirrus clouds high in the sky mean rain or snow may be coming later.

A big cumulonimbus cloud means that there may be a thunderstorm.

When tiny water droplets form close to the ground, this is called fog or mist.

This is the Golden Gate Bridge in California, USA. It is foggy there most of the time.

Icy crystals

When the air is very cold, the water in clouds freezes to make tiny ice crystals called snowflakes.

Most snowflakes have six points.

No two snowflakes are ever exactly the same shape.

This is what snowflakes
look like when they are
put under a microscope.

Icicles form in snowy weather when the
Sun shines onto snow on roofs or trees.

The snow melts.
Water drips down
into the cold shade,
where it freezes.

More water slowly
drips down and
freezes, forming lots
of icy 'fingers'.

Electric skies

Thunderstorms happen when a cumulonimbus cloud forms in the sky.

Strong winds inside the cloud swirl rain, snow and hailstones up and down.

This makes electricity build up. It escapes down to the ground as flashes of lightning.

Lightning sometimes hits trees and buildings on its way from the cloud to the ground.

Thunder is the sound that lightning makes when it heats up the air around it.

This type of lightning is called forked lightning.

You always see lightning before you hear thunder, because light travels faster than sound.

Great balls of ice

Hail forms inside giant thunderclouds, so you often get hailstorms at the same time as thunder and lightning.

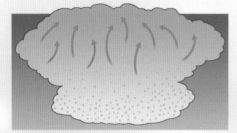

1. Water droplets get blown up to the top of the cloud by gusts of air.

2. The droplets freeze. They drop down and a layer of water forms around them.

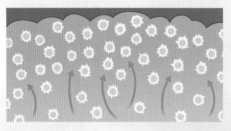

3. The hail is blown up to the top of the cloud again and the layer of water freezes.

4. This happens again and again until the hail gets too heavy and falls from the sky.

If a hailstone is cut in half, its layers look a bit like those in an onion.

This is the biggest hailstone ever. It fell in Nebraska, USA in 2003.

It is shown here
at just over half its actual size.

Wild wind

Wind is moving air. It happens when hot air rises and cold air rushes in to take its place.

The strength of the wind is measured on a scale from 1 to 12.

A force 2 breeze dries the clothes on a clothesline.

A force 5 wind blows the leaves from the trees.

A force 9 wind is a severe gale. It can blow tiles from roofs.

A force 12 wind is a hurricane. It can destroy houses.

A hurricane begins when hot air rises quickly over the sea and starts to spin. This causes a violent storm with heavy rain.

When a hurricane reaches land, huge waves and strong winds batter the coast.

The Ancient Greeks believed that the wind was the breath of the Gods.

17

Terrible twisters

Tornadoes are violent, whirling winds. They are sometimes called twisters.

A tornado is like a giant vacuum cleaner. It sucks things up from the ground.

1. The air inside a thundercloud slowly begins to spin around and around.

2. The air spins faster and faster. The cloud begins to change shape.

3. Warm air is sucked up into the cloud. It becomes shaped like a funnel.

4. The cloud touches the ground and as it moves, it destroys everything in its path.

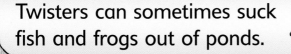

Twisters can sometimes suck fish and frogs out of ponds.

Weather scientists

Scientists measure the weather and then tell us what they think the weather will be like.

Wind speed and rain are measured at weather stations all over the world.

Special planes fly into clouds to measure how much water is in them.

Satellites in space take pictures of clouds and storms on Earth.

Some people think that cows
lie down when it is about to rain.

Weather balloons
are sent high into
the sky to measure
the air temperature.

The scientists put
together all this
information to make
a weather forecast.

The white, swirling cloud below is a
hurricane in the Atlantic Ocean.

Animal magic

Weather doesn't just affect people, it affects the way animals behave too.

For example, the fur of a snowshoe hare changes from brown to white for the winter.

The hare can't be spotted in the snow by eagles that hunt it.

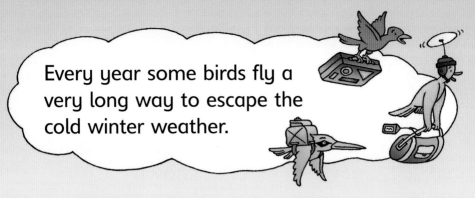

Every year some birds fly a very long way to escape the cold winter weather.

Some animals, like dormice, sleep through the long, cold winter. This is called hibernation.

When it gets colder, a dormouse eats lots of fruit and seeds.

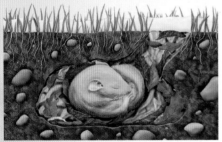

It makes a snug nest underground or in a tree and goes to sleep.

Six months later, it wakes up, ready for the summer ahead.

Hot and cold

Some places have such extreme weather that not many people or animals live there.

The Sahara Desert in Africa is one of the hottest and driest places on Earth.

Camels can live here because they can survive without water for a long time.

Under the hot sun, desert rocks become so hot that you could fry an egg on them!

Antarctica is the coldest place in the world.

Penguins are one of the few animals that are able to live there.

They huddle close together to keep warm in the winter.

Weird weather

In some parts of the world the weather makes odd things happen.

Some people think that strange clouds like this one look like spaceships.

It is called a lenticular cloud. They usually form near mountains.

Red raindrops sometimes fall from the sky.

Winds pick up red sand from African deserts and carry it across the sea.

The sand mixes with droplets of water in the clouds to make the red rain.

A hailstone with a turtle inside once fell from a thundercloud in Mississippi, USA!

Heating up?

Many scientists think that the Earth's atmosphere is slowly getting warmer.

The air in the atmosphere acts like a blanket to keep the Earth warm.

When fuels like oil and coal are burned, lots of gases are released into the air.

The atmosphere is getting warmer because the gases trap heat from the Sun.

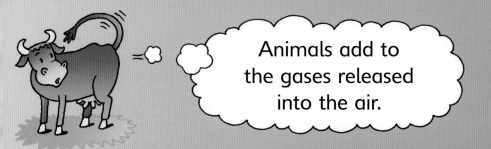

Animals add to the gases released into the air.

If the Earth gets warmer, the weather will change. In cold places, ice and snow would melt and could cause massive floods.

Hundreds of years from now, all this ice might have melted.

Glossary of weather words

Here are some of the words in this book you might not know. This page tells you what they mean.

 droplet - a tiny drop of water. Water droplets join together to make clouds.

 ice crystal - a frozen drop of water. Snowflakes are ice crystals.

 lightning - a flash of light from a thundercloud.

 hailstone - a lump of ice formed inside a thundercloud.

 hurricane - a fierce storm. These are also known as typhoons or cyclones.

 weather station - a place where scientists measure the weather.

 weather forecast - a report about what the weather is going to be like.

Websites to visit

You can visit exciting websites to find out more about weather.

To visit these websites, go to the Usborne Quicklinks Website at **www.usborne.com/quicklinks** Read the internet safety guidelines, and then type the keywords "**beginners weather**".

The websites are regularly reviewed and the links in Usborne Quicklinks are updated. However, Usborne Publishing is not responsible, and does not accept liability, for the content or availability of any website other than its own. We recommend that children are supervised while on the internet.

This child is wearing waterproof clothes to keep dry in the rain.

Index

air, 4, 5, 6, 10, 13, 14, 16, 17, 19, 21, 28, 29

animals, 22-23, 24, 25, 27, 29

Antarctica, 25

atmosphere, 5, 28

clouds, 4, 5, 6, 7, 8-9, 10, 12, 14, 19, 20, 21, 26, 27, 30

cold, 10, 11, 16, 23, 25, 29

fog, 4, 8, 9

hail, 4, 12, 14-15, 27, 30

heat, 4, 13, 16, 17, 24, 28

hibernation, 23

hurricanes, 16, 17, 21, 30

icicles, 11

lightning, 12-13, 14, 30

people, 24

rain, 4, 7, 9, 12, 17, 20, 21, 27

Sahara Desert, 24

satellites, 20

snow, 3, 4, 9, 10-11, 12, 22, 29

snowflakes, 10-11, 30

sun, 4, 6, 11, 24, 28

thunderstorms, 9, 12-13

tornadoes, 18-19

water cycle, 6-7

weather forecast, 21, 30

weather scientists, 20-21

wind, 4, 12, 16-17, 18, 20

Acknowledgements

Photographic manipulation by Nick Wakeford
With thanks to Stephanie Turnbull

Photo credits

The publishers are grateful to the following for permission to reproduce material:

Cover © Kent Wood/ Science Photo Library; **1** © Digital Archive Japan/Alamy; **2-3** © Jose Luis Pelaez, Inc./CORBIS; **8-9** © Ed Pritchard/Getty Images; **10-11** © Bettman/CORBIS; **13** © A. T. Willett/Alamy; **15** © Quilla Ulmer/Jim Reed Photography/Science Photo Library; **17** © Warren Faidley/CORBIS; **18-19** © Eric Meola/Getty Images; **20-21** © Orbimage/Science Photo Library; **22** © T. Kitchin & V. Hurst/Photoshot; **24-25** © Martin Harvey/Photoshot; **26-27** © Magrath/Folsom/Science Photo Library; **29** © Paul A. Souders/CORBIS; **31** © Christopher Furlong/Getty Images.